Connecting Cultures Through Family and Food

The Italian Family Table

by Diane Bailey

The Italian Family Table

By Diane Bailey

MASON CREST

Mason Crest
450 Parkway Drive, Suite D
Broomall, PA 19008
www.masoncrest.com

Printed and bound in the United States of America.

First printing
9 8 7 6 5 4 3 2 1

Series ISBN: 978-1-4222-4041-0
Hardback ISBN: 978-1-4222-4046-5
EBook ISBN: 978-1-4222-7744-7

Produced by Shoreline Publishing Group LLC
Santa Barbara, California
Editorial Director: James Buckley Jr.
Designer: Tom Carling
Production: Patty Kelley
www.shorelinepublishing.com
Cover: caracterdesign/iStock.com

Library of Congress Cataloging-in-Publication Data
Names: Bailey, Diane, 1966- author. Title: The Italian family table / by Diane Bailey.
Description: Broomall, PA : Mason Crest, 2018. | Series: Connecting cultures through family and food | Includes bibliographical references and index.
Identifiers: LCCN 2017053428| ISBN 9781422240465 (hardback) | ISBN 9781422240410 (series) | ISBN 9781422277447 (ebook)
Subjects: LCSH: Cooking, Italian--Juvenile literature. | Italian Americans--Food--Juvenile literature. | Food habits--Italy--Juvenile literature. | Italy--Social life and customs--Juvenile literature. | United States--Emigration and immigration--Juvenile literature.
Classification: LCC TX723 .B2326 2018 | DDC 641.5945--dc23 LC record available at https://lccn.loc.gov/2017053428

QR Codes disclaimer:

You may gain access to certain third party content ("Third-Party Sites") by scanning and using the QR Codes that appear in this publication (the "QR Codes"). We do not operate or control in any respect any information, products, or services on such Third-Party Sites linked to by us via the QR Codes included in this publication, and we assume no responsibility for any materials you may access using the QR Codes. Your use of the QR Codes may be subject to terms, limitations, or restrictions set forth in the applicable terms of use or otherwise established by the owners of the Third-Party Sites. Our linking to such Third-Party Sites via the QR Codes does not imply an endorsement or sponsorship of such Third-Party Sites, or the information, products, or services offered on or through the Third-Party Sites, nor does it imply an endorsement or sponsorship of this publication by the owners of such Third-Party Sites.

Contents

KEY ICONS TO LOOK FOR

Words to Understand: These words with their easy-to-understand definitions will increase the reader's understanding of the text, while building vocabulary skills.

Sidebars: This boxed material within the main text allows readers to build knowledge, gain insights, explore possibilities, and broaden their perspectives by weaving together additional information to provide realistic and holistic perspectives.

Educational Videos: Readers can view videos by scanning our QR codes, providing them with additional educational content to supplement the text. Examples include news coverage, moments in history, speeches, iconic moments, and much more!

Text-Dependent Questions: These questions send the reader back to the text for more careful attention to the evidence presented here.

Research Projects: Readers are pointed toward areas of further inquiry connected to each chapter. Suggestions are provided for projects that encourage deeper research and analysis.

Series Glossary of Key Terms: This back-of-the-book glossary contains terminology used throughout this series. Words found here increase the reader's ability to read and comprehend higher-level books and articles in this field.

Introduction

People are always looking for ways to stay young—they stick to a healthy diet, exercise regularly, and get plenty of sleep. No strategy works forever, but the Italians may have found the best one yet: Enjoy your dinner! An Italian saying goes, "*A tavola non si invecchia.*" In English that means, "At the table, no one grows old." Maybe that's why Italians like to spend hours lingering over their meals.

Italians have a long history of having not only an appetite for food, but for life as well. Italy produced the famous explorers Christopher Columbus, Marco Polo, and Amerigo Vespucci (for whom the Americas were named). The Renaissance—a time that put new emphasis on art, science, and culture—started in Italy in the 1300s. During the Renaissance, a period of a few centuries following the Middle Ages in Europe, Michelangelo painted the ceiling of the Sistine Chapel in Vatican City (in Rome), and Leonardo da Vinci painted the *Mona Lisa*, probably the most famous painting in the world. The musical form of opera was born in Florence, Italy. And the Italian scientist Galileo Galilei advocated a controversial idea (at the time, anyway): that the Earth revolved around the Sun.

At the time, most Italians did not believe (or even understand) that idea, and most of them probably did not care one way or the other. To them, the Sun and the Earth worked in a partnership to do the most important job: grow food. For any Italian—peasant or

king—food was the very center of life.

Centuries after the Renaissance, when Italians began moving away from the country looking for better opportunities, they took a few *lira*, some changes of clothes, and maybe a jar of tomatoes or a bottle of olive oil carefully packed among their belongings. They could not take all of Italy with them, but they could take a taste that would bring them back to its sunny fields, no matter where they landed.

Getting Here

A t the end of the 19th century, smoke was rising from the face of the Earth around the world. It billowed into the air from engines that powered trains, mining equipment, and factories. The advanced technology of the Industrial Revolution was changing the world. Railroad tracks were being laid with incredible speed, connecting the coasts of America and the countries of Europe. Cities grew up around factories that employed thousands of workers, churning out everything from cloth to steel.

In Italy, though, there wasn't much coal or petroleum to feed the hungry ma-

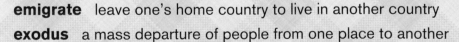

Words to Understand

emigrate leave one's home country to live in another country

exodus a mass departure of people from one place to another

exploited unfairly benefit from someone else's work

immigrants people who have left their home country and moved to another

unification the process of making several independent states into a single political whole

Italy at the turn of the 19th century was a rural nation, with small towns focused on farming, fishing, and family life.

chinery of the Industrial Revolution. Even by the turn of the 20th century, most people lived in rural areas, growing crops and raising animals to feed their families. For the nation's poor people, those were tough times. As countries like the United States, Britain, Canada, and Australia were leading the way into a new economy, many Italians were getting left behind.

Looking for a Better Way

Before 1860, Italy was not the country we recognize today. Instead, it was a collection of nation-states, each with its own government. But there were efforts to stitch all these different parts into a single whole. After decades of wars and political upheaval, by 1871 the many different regions were finally united into Italy.

As this new nation established itself over the next two decades, standards of living varied widely. Some citizens, especially in the north, were relatively well off. Others struggled to get by. And many, especially in the south, were desperately, crushingly poor. They were overwhelmingly peasants, living off the land. That's always a life of hard work, often at the mercy of the weather. There are good years and

Here's Milan, Italy, in the late 1800s, a city still far from industrial modernization.

Italy has a wide variety of terrain, from mountains in the north, to foothills farther south, and to beaches and Mediterranean climates.

bad. But in southern Italy, bad was outpacing good. And bad was getting worse.

Peasants in favor of **unification** had hoped that the new political structure would bring fairer laws. Instead, the new government was levying high taxes on the people who could least afford to pay them. Meanwhile, olives and grapes, two crops that were important to the country's agricultural industry, were suffering from attacks of disease and insects. Farmers who grew citrus fruits like oranges and lemons were competing with new suppliers in the United States. And Italy's population was growing, meaning more hungry children with less food to feed them.

In some places, women were mixing plaster from the walls in with their flour to make the bread dough stretch a little farther. Through it all, though, Italians clung to a sense of honor. Even when there was no food in the house, families would rattle the pots and pans and shake the tablecloths out the windows as if to rid them of crumbs, hoping to fool their neighbors into believing they were eating well. But it's only possible to pretend for so long, and by the 1870s, hundreds of thousands of Italians were looking for a way out or a better life.

Thousands of Italians arrived in the late 1800s and early 1900s on ships steaming from European ports.

Not a Helping Hand

Some Italians came to their new homes with plans to meet family members who were already estab-lished there. These earlier immi-grants could help the new arrivals find jobs and places to live. But many did not have even that much of a safety net. They stepped off the boat with no knowledge of the language, culture, or geography of the country. Needing a job quickly, they often turned to a *padrone*. The word is related to "patron," which means someone who will help. Unfortunately, many padrones—often other Italians—were less interested in helping immigrants than in helping themselves. They **exploited** new immigrants, promising to find them jobs, but charging high fees for their "help." Some of the jobs did not materialize, or paid less than was promised. A lot of new immigrants basically worked as servants, forced to pay off their padrone before they could move on.

Starting Fresh

In the years between Italian unification and the outbreak of World War I in 1914, it's estimated that about 16 million Italians **emigrated** to other countries. This period is sometimes called the great wave of immigra-tion, but it wasn't the first **exodus**. In the half-century before unification, thousands of Italians—mostly from northern Italy—also left the country.

But the great wave consisted overwhelmingly of southern Italians. About a quarter of these **immigrants**—roughly four million—came to the United States. Although America was home to Irish, Polish, Greek, Jewish, and other immigrants, those from Italy were the largest group. The vast majority came on ships that sailed through Ellis Island in New York Harbor, where the Statue of Liberty greeted them. Most of them didn't stray too far from the northeastern states, settling in large cities such as New York, Boston, Philadelphia, and Chicago.

Part of the reason for that was that they could not afford to keep traveling. Most had very little money, and they needed jobs fast. The other reason was that the Industrial Revolution had shifted jobs from rural areas

Gnocchi Day

On any 29th of a month, Argentinians recognize gnocchi day. Gnocchi are dumplings made with potatoes and flour. They were introduced to the country by Italians, along with pizza and pasta. The idea of gnocchi day comes from early immigrants, who usually received their pay on the first of the month. Many families were short on funds by the end of the month, just before payday. Inexpensive gnocchi made the perfect meal when money was at its tightest and the cupboard shelves held little. Today, the tradition continues in the homes of later-generation Italians and in restaurants, which sometimes serve nothing except gnocchi on this day. It's believed to bring good luck, and in families who aren't strapped for cash, it's customary for everyone to get a little money under their plates, too.

Italians at Ellis Island

into the cities. In the northeast, many Italians worked in textile mills, or on construction and public works projects, such as building bridges or maintaining sewers.

However, some immigrants made their way farther west, where they were employed by the railroad, or worked in coal and copper mines. And still others ventured south, where they found work in agriculture.

North and South

The United States was a prime destination for millions of Italians, but some of the Italian emigrants also settled in other places. South America, particularly Argentina and Brazil, attracted many. Argentina had a strong economy fed by both agriculture and technological developments from the Industrial Revolution. Italians who moved to Argentina could find work fairly easily. Plus, they were busiest during the Argentine summer (the growing season), which corresponded to winter in the

Northern Hemisphere. Since the goal of many immigrants was to earn money to send back to family members who had remained in the old country, being able to provide income during the harder months of Italy's winter was a bonus.

Brazil, meanwhile, had a burgeoning business in coffee, which was called "green gold." The government of Brazil actively recruited immigrants to work on coffee plantations in southeastern Brazil, even paying their way to get there. Unfortunately, working conditions could be horrendous, with immigrants toiling as virtual slaves. In 1902 the Italian government passed a law forbidding Brazil to "buy" immigrants by paying their expenses to relocate. Many Italians also got fed up and left. Some returned

Plantations in Brazil were the destination for some Italian workers, who often faced harsh conditions and a lack of freedoms.

to Italy, and others re-emigrated to countries such as Argentina, Uruguay, and the United States.

These few intense years of immigration, however, would have a lasting effect on the cultures of both Argentina and Brazil. Both still have significant populations of Italians, and their influence is evident in everything from language and music to festivals and food.

A Temporary Solution

A year or two, maybe even just a few months: the timetable for Italian immigrants to live abroad wasn't an exact one, but it did have an end. Leaving their homeland was a temporary solution. They wanted to earn money for their families at home and get some financial security. Then they would go back.

About half of Italian immigrants stuck with their original plans and returned to Italy. But the other half decided to stay. They weren't living in luxury, but for the most part, they were living a lot better than they had in Italy. They built new lives, and gradually, as they could afford it, they sent for other family members to join them.

By the early 1900s, when this photo was taken, New York's Little Italy was a bustling place.

Josephine Calloway immigrated to the United States from Sicily in 1922, to join her parents who had come earlier. Still living with family in Italy, she wasn't ready to go. "I wrote them a letter, when I was about fifteen years old. I asked them not to beg for me to come to America yet. I wanted to get my degree first," she said in a 1986 interview for an oral history project. But her father had other ideas. If he waited until Josephine was 16, he could not legally claim her. So he surprised her by showing up in Italy and knocking on her door late one night. Soon after, Josephine was on her way to the United States.

Italian Americans and the wider population still enjoy specialty markets such as this one in New York City with a focus on Italian food.

Even though immigrants were leaving Italy, they were not abandoning it. Instead, they saw emigrating as a way to save their Italian lifestyle. At home, they were poor and suffering. Abroad, they had a better chance to live in relative comfort—the Italian way. They took with them their language, their lifestyles, and their love of food!

Text-Dependent Questions:

1. About how many Italian immigrants settled in the United States between 1861 and 1914?

2. What are two factors that contributed to the poverty in southern Italy in the second half of the 19th century?

3. Why was Argentina another prime destination for Italian immigrants?

Research Project:

Some Italian immigrants traveled several times between America and Italy. They were called "birds of passage." Find out more about these immigrants. Why did they go back and forth?

APPETIZER

The evening meal is a long, leisurely affair in an Italian household, and it starts with the *antipasti*, which means "before the meal." The small bites of food that make up antipasti are usually cold and colorful, and there's a lot of variety. Diners can snack their way through it all, relaxing and talking. You don't have to be hungry to enjoy antipasti—it's the appetizer's job to get everyone's taste buds and appetites ready for the later courses. It's easy to fill up on antipasti alone, but save some room. A traditional Italian meal has four or five courses, so there's lots more to come!

Different regions of Italy have different specialties that are used as antipasti, but most feature cured meats or fish, and an assortment of fruits and vegetables. Thin slices of prosciutto and pancetta might be served in individual rolls, or with a bit of a fruit or vegetable tucked inside. Both are types of cured pork, but they're not the same. Prosciutto is an Italian ham, while pancetta is more like bacon.

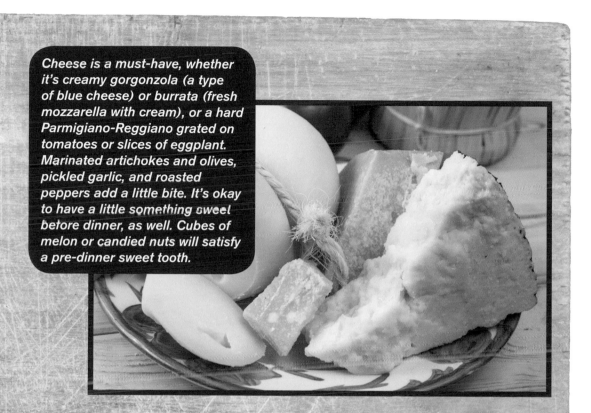

Cheese is a must-have, whether it's creamy gorgonzola (a type of blue cheese) or burrata (fresh mozzarella with cream), or a hard Parmigiano-Reggiano grated on tomatoes or slices of eggplant. Marinated artichokes and olives, pickled garlic, and roasted peppers add a little bite. It's okay to have a little something sweet before dinner, as well. Cubes of melon or candied nuts will satisfy a pre-dinner sweet tooth.

A great way to combine a lot of flavors is with bruschetta. This can be made to the cook's preference (and whatever's in the fridge), but a basic recipe is just fresh tomatoes and basil tossed with olive oil and a splash of balsamic vinegar, spooned on top of toasted bread. Take the same ingredients, and serve it on slabs of mozzarella cheese and you've got a caprese salad.

Settling In

Josephine Calloway had a problem with her eye, and after arriving at **Ellis Island** in New York Harbor, she was put in the hospital wing. Her brother, housed nearby in the men's wing, called to her one day while they were outside in the yard, and they met at the fence that separated the two wings. He had an apple he wanted to give her—a large one that could be bought for five cents. "He wanted to put it through the bars, but it wouldn't go through!," Josephine remembers. "And he didn't have a knife so he couldn't cut it."

It was a frustrating experience for her, but many other immigrants were luckier.

Words to Understand

Ellis Island   US arrival point in New York Harbor for millions of immigrants, mostly from Europe

kneading   squeezing and smashing dough to prepare it for baking

staples   basic ingredients of a family's food, such as flour, eggs, milk, and bread

tenements   large apartment buildings with many units, often overcrowded with people

Today, the buildings at Ellis Island that once welcomed tens of thousands of immigrants now welcome tourists who want to learn the story of the place.

Unlike the places they'd left, where food was expensive and often scarce, on Ellis Island they were greeted with free coffee and doughnuts, milk, and sandwiches. It's true the sandwiches were made from soft, sliced white bread, not the heartier loaves Italians were used to. A lot of immigrants found it a poor excuse for bread. Still, they took what was offered. After all, who could argue with a sign that read: *No Charge for Meals Here*.

Land of Plenty

Depending on the region they came from, Italians had certain foods that were central to their diets. Some preferred more pork or more fish, or they would choose barley over corn. Some always made certain cookies on holidays, or swore by a certain way of preparing sausage.

Making pasta from scratch is actually pretty easy and worth a try!

The food they ate, and the traditions surrounding it, made up the Italian "foodways."

Americans had very different foodways, but what made the biggest impression on Italian immigrants was not the type of food or how it was eaten. It was the amount. America was indeed the "land of plenty." Not only was there more of everything, but it was cheaper, too. Many immigrants were astonished to learn that Americans could afford to drink coffee every morning and eat meat every evening. In Italy, flour was expensive, so people mixed it with ground corn, oats, chickpeas, barley, chestnuts, or potatoes before they made their bread. In America, the price of flour was low enough that even the working classes could eat bread made entirely with wheat flour.

Even pasta was easy to come by. In Italy, it was reserved for special occasions—unless you were rich. Not only was the price of flour high, but making homemade pasta was a lot of work. Mixing and **kneading** the dough, rolling it out, adding the filling to individual ravioli or hanging thin strands of vermicelli from a rack so they didn't get tangled—who had time for all that?

By the turn of the 20th century, things had changed. New machinery and methods allowed vendors to mass-produce pasta, as well as to dry it so it could be more easily stored and transported. A walk through an Italian neighborhood in New York around the turn of the century meant coming upon several pasta shops—now with the vermicelli hanging in the windows to attract customers.

Such extravagance was unheard of in Italy. "Who could afford to eat spaghetti more than once a week [in Italy]? In America no one starved," remembered one Sicilian woman who immigrated to New York. "Our *paesani* [fellow Italians] here in America ate to their heart's delight till they were belching like pigs. [They] dumped mountains of uneaten food out the windows."

Stretching a Dollar

Okay, dumping food out the windows might be an exaggeration, but life in America was definitely easier on the wallet. In Italy, the average Italian peasant spent about 75 percent of his income on food. In America, it was only 25 percent. Italians weren't as well-to-do as other Americans—or even some other immigrants—but their situation was so improved that it didn't seem to matter. The Sicilian woman added, "We were not poor in America; we just had a little less than the others."

And "a little less" was still enough. With hardship fresh on their minds,

80-2 STREET VENDER, ITALIAN FEAST

From the beginning, Italian immigrants have been involved in selling food.

immigrant Italians were not wasteful. They were good at making the most out of what they had. In general, it was the job of women to shop and cook. A "good" wife and mother was one who knew how to squeeze every penny out of the family budget, and how to stretch the food in the pantry to feed a growing family.

Most immigrants faced a very different lifestyle than they had known back in Italy. Rather than growing food, they bought it. Instead of living in rural areas, many now lived in cities, often crowded into **tenements** with several people living in one room.

But however much space they had, they were creative in using every inch. Even living in small apartments, many found a little room to grow an Italian garden on the roof or fire escape. It might not be much, just a few tomatoes, peppers, and herbs, but every little bit helped—both with the budget and with preserving the Italian way of doing things.

They were savvy shoppers, but they were not stingy. One study showed that more than any other immigrant group, Italians were willing to spend

A Woman's Place...and a Man's

Men in Italian families left the main cooking chores to women, but that did not mean they had no interest in food—far from it! Most early immigrants were single men who'd done their own shopping and cooking. During that time, they learned their own tricks and preferences, and they didn't abandon them once women showed up. While the women were in the kitchen making bread or stews, the men might be found in the cellar, salting their own cuts of meat or making homemade wine. Or they might be offering advice to their wives. Edith Abbott, a scholar from the early 20th century, noted, "Italian men have a lively interest in food, many of them know a good deal about it, are good cooks and better critics."

their money on food. After buying **staples** like flour and vegetables, they also earmarked a large portion of the family budget for meat or poultry, as well as for expensive foods imported directly from Italy, such as olive oil. Food kept the Italian family tight-knit and happy, so buying the good stuff came at a price they happily paid.

Coming Together

Imagine walking through a large, unfamiliar city. You don't know your way around. You don't speak the language and can't read the signs. But you know what broccoli and cauliflower look like, and you know the pushcart vendor selling those vegetables is always stationed at a particular corner in the city. The man selling your favorite fruit is just across

As with many immigrants, Italian Americans created clubs, societies, and organizations to help them retain connections to their homeland.

the street. The small child tugging at your arm wants a *dolce*—but she'll have to wait: The cart with ice cream is still two blocks on, and anyway, a sweet treat comes as a reward only *after* the daily shopping is finished!

As the number of immigrants swelled, it wasn't long before American cities began to have entire neighborhoods devoted to people from one area. Neighborhoods called "Little Italy" were vibrant places filled with businesses catering to Italians. These markets were important places to immigrants. They helped them navigate large cities, connect with others, and buy food that was authentically Italian.

Not that it was all the same. In Italy, historian Robert Orsi reported in the 2015 PBS documentary *The Italian Americans*, "Each little village had its own saint, its own language, its own dialect, its own cuisine." The same thing happened on the streets of major cities where Italians came to live. The food for sale on one block might be

 ## The Sound of the Bells

Even after the unification of Italy in 1871, Italians still felt fierce loyalty to the particular region they came from. They identified themselves as being from places such as Sicily (above), Calabria, or Campania, not just Italy. Even within those regions, they were from smaller towns or villages. Most had a bell tower, called a *campanile* in Italian. The bells were rung to notify people that it was time to pray or come to church, or to mark a special occasion such as a wedding or death. The Italian concept of *campanilismo* describes loyalty to a particular place, referring to the area that was reached by the sound of the bells. Italian immigrants carried this tradition into their new countries, with *campanilismo* now tied to a certain block within a large city.

An Italian bakery is a delight for the senses, especially for the smells!

noticeably different from that being offered two streets over. Depending on where they came from, one baker might offer bread that was round and puffy; another had loaves that were long and flat; still another shaped his into rings and crescents. Was the bread white, or more yellow in color? Was it flavored with fennel, or olives, or wine? Must it be eaten the day it was baked, or was it even better a day or two later? All these choices were based on the region of Italy from which the baker's family had come.

Michael Parenti remembered his father hard at work making bread. "[It] was the same bread that had been made in Gravina [a town in southern Italy] for generations," he wrote in his book *Dirty Truths*. "The secret of the bread had been brought by my grandfather all the way from the Mediterranean to Manhattan, down into the tenement basement."

Time for Celebration

Most Italians were Catholic, and especially important in their religion was the celebration of certain feast days, or *festa*, during which they would honor a particular saint.

Each year on July 16, for example, New York Italians turned out by the thousands for the festa celebrating Our Lady of Mt. Carmel. They paraded through the streets carrying a statue of the Madonna, eating the whole time from the pushcarts that crowded the streets. There were boiled beans; pies with tomatoes, red peppers, and garlic; and mounds of pasta. To satisfy the sweet tooth, there were balls of fried dough coated in sugar, nuts, and raisins; and of course, ice cream, which cost just five cents for a "jumbo" portion in 1935.

New York Italian festival food

Mulberry Street in New York City is the heart of Little Italy and here is the site of an annual festival attended by thousands.

Food also featured heavily in the Feast of Saint Joseph, held in March. The feast dates back to the Middle Ages, when peasants believed that Saint Joseph had answered their prayers for rain to end a drought. They showed their gratitude with an enormous feast. For one Southern Italian immigrant in Chicago, the day took on another meaning. In the 1940s, Mrs. Carl Gangitano asked Saint Joseph to make sure her son returned safely from World War II. When her prayer was answered, she kept her promise to the saint by serving up a traditional feast, which took her and her four daughters a month to prepare!

Whether it was a holiday feast or just an ordinary weekday dinner, food was the glue that bound together the Italian family—and the whole community. It fed their bodies, and it nourished their souls. It was a way they stayed connected to one another. In some ways, though, it also separated them from mainstream society—at least at first.

Text-Dependent Questions:

1. In Italy, what ingredients, besides flour, did cooks add to their bread? Why?

2. Many Italians were used to living in rural areas and growing their own food. How did they adapt once they moved to large cities?

3. What is *campanilismo*?

Research Project:

Many immigrants to the United States lived in tenements, a type of poor, crowded housing. Find out more about what it was like to live in a tenement in a major city such as New York or Philadelphia.

FIRST COURSE

Think of the *primo* ("first") course in an Italian meal as the bridge between the antipasti and the main course still to come. Portions are generally on the small side. Whereas Americans will fill up on a huge dish of pasta as the main meal, Italians are more likely to have a serving that's about the size of their fist.

Traditionally, most Italians just ate their pasta plain, maybe with a light coating of butter or olive oil. Red sauce came late to the Italian table, but when it did, it made a splash. Sometimes called "Sunday gravy," this tomato-based sauce included plenty of meat and spices and took hours to prepare. It was a good cook's signature dish. But if there wasn't enough time to spend hours over the stove, a marinara sauce with tomatoes and onions could be whipped up quickly and would fill in nicely.

No matter how much you love pasta, it's nice to switch it up sometimes, and other first course dishes include risotto, a creamy dish made from rice, or gnocchi (potato dumplings). Polenta—corn meal—was traditionally a food for peasants, because it was so inexpensive. It could be soft and creamy, like oatmeal, or fried and served in slabs, like hard pancakes.

Feeling carbed up? Soup is a way to de-starch and add some versatility to the first course. A classic minestrone does not even have a set recipe—it's just Italian for "vegetable soup," so whatever produce happens to be on hand—plus cannellini beans—is what goes into the pot. And when it's time to really stretch the family budget, a ribollita ("reboiled" stew) uses up leftovers (you can start with yesterday's minestrone) and adds cubes of bread to bulk it up.

Connecting

What's in your lunchbox? One Italian immigrant boy distinctly remembered what his mother packed: a sandwich of fried peppers and onions, dripping with oil and smelling of garlic. Delicious? Maybe. But he couldn't possibly be seen with it. "Such a sandwich would certainly ruin my reputation; I could not take it to school," he remembered, as reported by Simone Cinotto in *The Italian American Table*. Instead, he used the money he earned from shining shoes to buy food that was more like what his classmates brought. And *still* he wasn't done with the offensive sandwich: "My God, what a problem it was to dispose of it, for I was taught never to throw away bread."

The cultural differences between Italians and Americans were everywhere, from

Words to Understand

assimilate   change yourself to mix into a new culture or situation

oppression   a system that forces people to follow strict rules or a system that restricts freedoms

rations   food or meals supplied by an army to its soldiers

Hungry yet? This classic Italian combination of fresh tomoatoes, mozzarella cheese, and lettuce makes for a healthy and tasty lunch.

their ideas of raising children to their taste in food. Immigrants struggled to find a balance in their new homes. Should they try to fit in? Or should they remain true to their Italian roots as much as possible?

Finding a Place

People born in America often had conflicting attitudes toward immigrants. On the one hand, they welcomed the inexpensive labor provided by immigrants. On the other hand, they usually saw immigrants as inferior to themselves. Not only had they not been born here, but they often had customs that seemed strange.

Italians were looked down upon for several reasons. Their darker coloring made them look different—and to some, threatening. Most

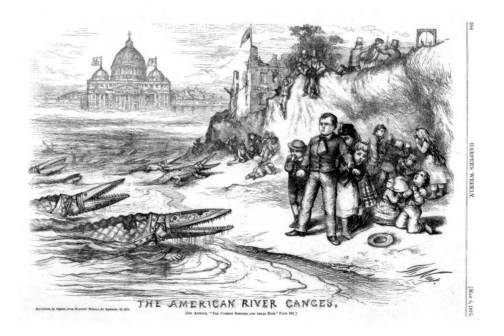

THE AMERICAN RIVER GANGES,

Anti-immigrant sentiment against Italians often centered on their Roman Catholic faith. The "alligators" are wearing hats like the pope's.

were Catholic, not Protestant like the majority of Americans. They lived primarily in large cities, which was at odds with the rural tradition of America (even though many immigrants had come from rural areas in Italy). They ate strange food, including lots of garlic, which was far too strong, smelly, and foreign to native-born Americans. Crimes were often blamed on Italians, especially because of their historic association with gangs called *mafia*. In truth, Italians were no more likely to be criminals than anyone else.

In the early 1900s, social workers tried to **assimilate** immigrants and make them more "American." At school, Italian children's long names, often crowded with vowels, were shortened and simplified. Speaking Italian was discouraged. The whole family's diets were examined—and usually came up short. Italians found a cup of coffee and maybe a sweet treat the perfect breakfast, but it was unacceptable to social workers. Instead, they suggested oatmeal. Oatmeal? Italians turned up their noses at that suggestion. In Italy, that was pig food! John Mariani writes in *How Italian Food Conquered the World* that one social worker from the time reported, "Not yet Americanized. Still eating Italian food."

Everyone in their Seats

Family comes first. That was the unofficial Italian motto. Decades of **oppression** by authorities in Italy had taught people to rely only on their own family members, and they did not trust outsiders. Immigrants carried this attitude with them. They might be far from home, but they believed that if they stuck together, they would be okay.

Unless they had to be away for school or work, it was expected that all family members show up for meals. This gave everyone a chance to catch up on what was happening in each other's lives. The dinner table was a place where they could escape the stress of being immigrants and the judgment of others. Here, they could just be Italian.

The dinner schedule usually was set by the man of the house. One immigrant remembers that other members of the family had better not be late. Once his father had sat down and was ready to eat, the door was locked. Anyone who was not in their place went without dinner.

Sundays, in particular, were days for enthusiastic eating. As one Sicilian immigrant recalled, not only would there be soup and salad, as on a regular day, but also three courses of meat, an assortment of vegetables,

A big Italian feast has plenty of food—and plenty of choices—for everyone.

California Dreaming

When Italians began arriving in the United States in the 1880s, many of them headed to California, where they went into business making wine from the grapes that grew so well in the California climate. Today, the vineyards in northern California are known all over the world for producing excellent wine, and many of the old, familiar companies bear the names of Italian immigrants who started them. Winemaking was a tradition in Italy, but history shows that most of the northern California

immigrants did not have that experience. Instead, they were shrewd enough to recognize an opening. Instead of producing light, white wines that were popular with Americans, they concentrated on the more robust red varieties that Italians liked. They also established shipping networks that stretched across the country, bringing their wine to large populations of Italians living in the Northeast.

and pastries and fruit to finish up. It was common for an Italian wife to rise early to start the "Sunday gravy," the tomato-and-meat sauce that would later go over the pasta.

Home-cooked dishes were the preferred items on the menu. First-generation immigrants, in particular, disliked prepared foods. Jerry Della Femina was a third-generation immigrant who grew up in Brooklyn. He remembers the time his mother bought a Betty Crocker apple pie mix.

(Betty Crocker wasn't actually a real person—she was a fictional house-wife made up by a food company. Her purpose was to put a friendly face on packaged food so that American housewives would buy it.)

When Della Femina's grandmother saw the pie mix, she was furious. She predicted the children would die if they ate it. His mother ignored her protests and made it anyway. "Whether it was voodoo or botulism [food-borne sickness], the entire family got deathly ill from the pie," he said, as Simone Cinotto recounted in *The Italian American Family Table*. "It was the last alien food to enter the house for a good ten years."

Best of Both Worlds

Italians liked to keep to themselves, and native citizens weren't always welcoming. That combination of factors kept the Italian community fairly isolated for years. But, put people together closely enough, for long enough, and eventually they rub off on each other. Little Italies around the world were hard places to resist. There were delicious smells coming from the kitchens of Italian restaurants; elaborate pastries displayed in the windows of the bakeries; and the red, green, and white colors of the Italian flag proudly displayed everywhere. It wasn't long before exploring Italian culture—and especially its food—was on the agenda of non-Italians.

Meanwhile, Italians were becoming more open to American food trends. Since meat was relatively inexpensive, they started using a lot more of it. Instead of a small piece of chicken as a rare treat, now they could have one that covered the entire plate! Meatballs, which used to be the size of marbles, swelled to the size of baseballs, and were served up with spaghetti—a combination unheard of in Italy. The notion of "Italian" food was really Italian-American food.

This statue of Ettore Boiardi stands outside a former Chef Boyardee factory in Milton, Pennsylvania.

Italian immigrant Ettore Boiardi opened a restaurant (named The Italian Immigrant) in Cleveland, Ohio, in 1926. There, his red sauces became so popular that customers started asking for portions to take home. Seeing an opportunity, Boiardi started canning his sauce and selling it. Later he added the spaghetti, too, so that anyone with a can opener and a stove could get a one-dish meal in the time it took to heat it up. He was clearly appealing to American tastes, and to make sure that he and his products didn't seem too foreign, he changed his name to Hector Boyardee so that Americans wouldn't trip over their tongues. By the 1930s, the US Army selected Chef Boyardee products to be one of the main **rations** for soldiers.

Through Thick and Thin

Got the munchies? A slice of bread with a scoop of tomato sauce and a bit of cheese is easy to put together, and it became popular among people living in the city of Naples, Italy, in the 19th century. Little did they know that within a century their snack—pizza—would take over the world's cuisine.

Few types of food are better known, or more loved. Part of the reason is that pizza can be eaten in so many different ways. The traditional triangle of ingredients—bread, cheese, and tomatoes—is just the beginning. Add some peppers? Sure! Pile on some pepperoni? Why not?

Pizza was still largely confined to Italian communities, even into the 1940s, but World War II changed that. US soldiers who had been stationed in Italy got used to eating pizza abroad, and when they came home they wanted more. Their demand for pizza helped jump-start the pizza revolu-

The story of pizza

tion that forever changed the way Americans eat. Bakers in Chicago took the thin crust typical in Italy and fattened it up into the thick, deep-dish pizza the city is known for today. The single slices on sale on the streets of Italy grew into enormous pies that could feed the whole family. Pizza has evolved so much that it's not even necessary to include the basic ingredients. It's not hard to find cheese-less or tomato-less versions—but at least the bread is still there!

Text-Dependent Questions:

1. What was one reason native-born Americans sometimes looked down on Italians?

2. What is "Sunday gravy"?

3. How did World War II help pizza become popular in the United States?

Research Project:

Italian food saw a lot of changes once it came to America. Find out more about different "Italian" dishes that were invented—or became popular—in America. Hint: *fettucine alfredo* is a good place to start.

SECOND COURSE

In a traditional Italian meal, after the primo course comes the *secondo*, which typically features a protein to build on the starchy filler of the first course. The secondo is either accompanied by, or closely followed by, the *contorno* course, usually made up of vegetables. That word is related to "contours" or "shapes," and literally means to "round out" the main course. And while Americans tend to eat their salad before their meals, Italians serve it during, or even after, the main course.

Decades ago, meat and poultry were expensive, so they weren't readily available to poorer people in Italy. Fish was also hard to come by except for those who lived by the water. As a result, meat was often stretched by making it only one of several ingredients in a stew or casserole. Cacciatore is a classic example. The word means "hunter" in Italian. This stew is made with onions, tomatoes, wine, and mushrooms. In America today, it's most often made with chicken (above), but traditionally this recipe features small game that hunters brought home, such as rabbit, quail, or pheasant.

Scaloppine is another popular way to prepare a variety of meats. Chicken, veal, pork, or fish could be cut into scaloppa (thin slices), then dusted with flour and fried in a pan. Piccatta (below), a type of scaloppine, was served with a light sauce made from white wine, lemon juice, and capers, while the heavier marsala featured red wine and mushrooms.

SECOND COURSE

Cooked properly, meat and fish do not need much accompaniment. They have all the flavor they need with just a squeeze of lemon and a sprig of parsley as a finish. One Italian restaurant owner complained that he couldn't serve food that way—it was too simple! Guests wanted something with more flair if they were going to pay restaurant prices. Over time, courses began to blend together. Instead of pasta followed by protein, now it was just one dish of spaghetti and meatballs, or linguine and clams (below), or rigatoni with sausage. Even the lowly polenta got served up with meat, sauce, and veggies and became a go-to dish at fancy restaurants.

Most Italians, however, preferred eating at home over eating out—Italian restaurants were actually geared more toward non-Italians. But everyone needs a quick bite out now and then, and when Italians ate out they might grab a muffaletta sandwich (right), made with layers of Italian cold cuts, or a Philly cheesesteak sandwich— thin-sliced beef topped with peppers and melted cheese. Both were invented by Italian immigrants looking for ways to provide a tasty, quick meal.

It's important to get off to a good start— especially in cooking. Soup, stew, sauce— whatever the end result, the first step is a soffritto. It's also called the "holy trinity" in Italian cooking because of its three ingredients, carrots, celery, and onions (heavy on the onions). These are gently cooked together until they soften and release their flavor. The soffritto base is just the beginning—good cooks then add their choice of garlic, tomatoes, and herbs to spice things up.

Reaching Back

By the 1960s and 1970s, Italian immigrants and their descendants in the United States were no longer seen as outsiders. Instead, they were people who had helped shape the nation into one that celebrated all cultures.

Their heritage was still proudly on display, though. In their homes, it wasn't uncommon to see an Italian flag flying right next to an American one. Family **heirlooms** from Italy sat next to souvenirs from American vacations. And for Janice Mancuso, an American first name came before her Italian surname. Mancuso was supposed to be named Jiavanna, after her grandmother. But there was no English equivalent for that name, so her parents chose the more American "Janice." Nev-

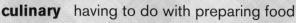
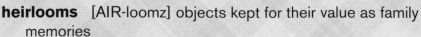

Words to Understand

culinary having to do with preparing food

heirlooms [AIR-loomz] objects kept for their value as family memories

matriarch a woman who is head of a large family

skewers long, thin, pointed sticks on which food is speared for grilling

Italian Americans happily celebrate their culture. Here, a building in New York's Little Italy is painted with the colors of the Italian flag.

Who Gives a Fig?

You might once have seen an odd sight on Italian farms—farmers burying fig trees. That may seem sound a little strange, but there was a reason for it. A century ago, when the first Italians arrived in the United States, they sometimes brought a fig sapling with them. Fig trees are common in southern Italy, and for poor people especially, the trees' fruit was a welcome part of their diet. But fig trees like warm, sunny weather, not the colder climate of much of the northeastern United States where Italian immigrants settled. To help the trees survive the winter, immigrants buried them underground. It's tough on the plants. They're bent sideways, and they must hold on by just a few of their strongest roots. But it's enough to get them through. Later generations of Italians are carrying on the tradition. Michele Vaccaro, who moved to America from Italy in 1976, said in a 2014 interview with NPR, "We cannot forget Italy. It's always in our blood. [This] keeps us in touch with our Italian heritage."

ertheless, Janice grew up immersed in her Italian heritage. Her father had immigrated with his family from Sicily to Brooklyn, New York, in the early 1930s, when he was eight years old, and Mancuso still remembers the authentic meals her grandmother prepared: "Although the grandchildren preferred meatballs and sausage, she kept her food traditions from the coast of Sicily by cooking *scungilli* [sea snails], *calamari* [squid], octopus, sardines, and *baccala* (salt-cured cod)." The food—and the memories that came with them—stuck with Janice. As an adult, she continues to promote Italian culture.

In Italian American kitchens all over the country, prized recipes were passed down to the next generations. Paul Nauta grew up in New Orleans, Louisiana. His grandparents came from Italy during the great wave of immigration at the turn of the 20th century. "Cookbooks from Italian matriarchs are some of the most strongly contested items upon the death of an Italian grandmother," he wrote in a 2016 blog post. "All my siblings and I have these, and we cherish them, particularly if they include recipes from the family or handwritten notes from 'Mamma.' In fact, we still criticize each other's dishes and argue about who cooks the most authentic food according to 'Mamma's' recipe."

Changing Tastes

The classic image of an Italian restaurant at the middle of the 20th century was one with red-and-white checkered tablecloths, bottles of red chianti wine (wrapped in straw to protect the bottle) on every

Pizza remains the most popular Italian addition to the American menu.

Pizza restaurants of every shape and size can be found around the United States and in many other countries.

table, and pictures of Italian landscapes on the walls. For the most part, the menu reflected a Southern Italian heritage—with a generous dose of Americanism. There were spaghetti and meatballs, pizza, hearty red sauces—and lots of garlic, which Americans had come to appreciate. Was it authentic? Well, it didn't exactly duplicate what Italians in Italy ate. But it *did* reflect how immigrants had changed the cuisine of their adopted country. By the second half of the 20th century, many Italians were eating food that had strong influences from American culture.

By the 1970s and 1980s, Italian restaurants were getting a makeover. Trade laws got less strict, which made imported Italian products less expensive. Pricey oil, vinegar, and cheeses started showing up on menus. And restaurants also started exploring the cuisine of Northern Italy more.

Marcella Hazan, who was born in a coastal town of north-central Italy, immigrated to New York City in the 1950s after getting married. Although she'd never cooked back home, she found out she had better learn quickly. "There I was, having to feed a young, hard-working husband who could deal cheerfully with most of life's ups and downs, but not with an indifferent meal," she remembered in her 1997 book *Marcella Cucina*. Hazan taught herself to cook, and made a name for herself writing cookbooks in the 1970s. She introduced ingredients that many Americans had never heard of, such as prosciutto, Parmigiano-Reggiano cheese, and balsamic vinegar.

Family Traditions

The Italian family can be sprawling and complicated, but there's one thing that's guaranteed to bring them together: the simple tradition of Sunday dinner.

Janice Mancuso remembers, "Every Sunday during my childhood and teenage years, a large pot of tomato sauce laden with meatballs, sausage, pieces of pork, and *braciole* [sliced meat], would simmer on the stove. Both my parents prepared our Sunday dinners—my mother made the meatballs and braciole; my father kept

Braciole can take a while to prepare, but its combination of savory tastes is worth it!

an eye on the simmering sauce and frequently stirred the pot."

It was a similar story in Guy Valponi's household. Looking for better jobs, his great-grandparents emigrated from Southern Italy to the Cleveland, Ohio, area in the 1910s. After several generations, his family still maintains several **culinary** traditions, including making *spiedini* (skewers) for the Easter holiday. These thin-cut steaks are stuffed with breadcrumbs,

 ## The Roseto Effect

Starchy pasta, fatty meat, and a few cannoli (cream-filled pastries) might be the perfect Italian meal, but nutritionists would argue that this cholesterol-clogged diet is not very healthy. So why did researchers in the 1960s find that Italian immigrants living in Roseto, Pennsylvania, had only half the rate of heart disease as other Americans? Certainly, drinking large amounts of red wine and smoking cigarettes wasn't helping either. Researchers came up with an explanation that had less to do with cholesterol than it did with community. This Italian enclave was very close-knit, and its people were comfortable and secure. Adriana Trigiani, an author whose father and grandfather were born in Roseto, observed, "They're not afraid about old age because they're going to live with their families. They know they'll never starve because the guy next door has a garden and a cow." A healthy diet is one thing, but in Roseto, it seemed a healthy attitude was just as important. In the PBS documentary *The Italian Americans*, one resident said, "Spaghetti is not the best thing for you all the time, but I tell you, if I'm gonna go, I'm gonna go with a meatball in my mouth!"

Italian food traditions

raisins, pine nuts, and Parmesan cheese, then placed on **skewers** with onions and grilled. When Valponi was growing up, it was tradition that only men were permitted to grill the spiedini, while the women stayed inside and readied the rest of the meal.

Alessandro Borgognone also sets aside Sundays for food and family. A second-generation Italian who runs a Japanese restaurant in New York, he's used to hungry diners. They come in every day of the week except Sunday. That day, he closes the restaurant—but it's hardly a day off! After an espresso—strong Italian coffee—to help him get going, Borgognone gets everything simmering on the stove and then makes a run to an authentic Sicilian pastry shop (he's half Sicilian) to get desserts for later. Then it's back home to ready the roasted peppers with capers and olives, the *salumi* (cold cuts made from pork) and the baccala (salted cod) with cherry tomatoes and potatoes served as antipasti.

Nothing makes Italian food better than eating it with your family.

At about two o'clock, the family gathers in the dining room to feast. "We make a classic Neapolitan dinner," Borgognone said in a 2014 interview with *The New York Times*. (The chef is half Neapolitan and half Sicilian.) "Pigskin braciola, pork rib, sometimes sausages. The meatballs are pan-fried, and have three meats. I mean, it's real. [But] you can't have it every Sunday because otherwise you'll drop dead."

In today's world, Italians have several ways of keeping their heritage alive. Tracing their family roots to past generations is popular. So is visiting Italy. Technology makes it easy to share stories through blogs or websites. But nothing beats the satisfaction of sharing a meal—or even just a cup of coffee and some *biscotti* (cookies). They might be homemade from a beloved grandmother's secret recipe, but it's fine to pick some up at the corner bakery, too. The important part isn't where they came from a few minutes ago—it's remembering the traditions that have kept Italian food alive for centuries.

Text-Dependent Questions:

1. What was one reason imported Italian ingredients began to be used more frequently in the 1970s and 1980s?

2. In Guy Valponi's family, what was notable about the tradition of grilling *spiedini*?

3. Researchers found that Italian residents of Roseto, Pennsylvania, had lower rates of heart disease than average. What reason did they give for this?

Research Project:

Pizza started in Naples, Italy, but it's now popular all over the world, with new versions that reflect the regions where it spread. Create your own pizza, using ingredients that are common in your area.

DESSERT

In the classic mobster movie *The Godfather*, one of the characters states, "Leave the gun. Take the cannoli." The movie portrays Italians as merciless killers and crime bosses—far from the truth of most Italians—but it gets the importance of food right! Cannoli are one of the best-known Italian desserts. Fried pastry dough is rolled into a tube, and then filled with a creamy paste of ricotta cheese and sugar. To get more fancy, add fruit, nuts, and chocolate, then sprinkle the whole thing with powdered sugar. Cannoli started as a special-occasion delicacy served just before the Catholic season of Lent, but it's evolved into an any-day treat.

Making pastries takes a lot of time and work, so immigrants who could afford it generally just bought them from the local baker. Early Italian bakeries made an astonishing variety of cookies, doughnuts, and cakes, often with a regional flair. There's biscotti, a cookie that's baked twice to make it dry and hard (and perfect for dipping in coffee), and crunchy-on-the-outside, chewy-on-the-inside brutti ma buoni, an almond meringue cookie. Oh, and about a hundred other varieties!

Sorbetto, *simply ice flavored with fruit, and gelato (similar to ice cream, but denser and not as rich) have been around for centuries in Italy, but some "classic" Italian desserts are a lot more recent. Today, most Italian restaurants feature* tiramisu, *which alternates layers of coffee-soaked ladyfingers (a cookie), and custard mixed with mascarpone cheese. It's delicious, but it wasn't until the 1960s that an Italian restaurateur invented this popular dessert, which quickly made its way onto menus across the world.*

Find Out More

Books

Aldridge, Rebecca. *Italian Americans*. New York: Chelsea House, 2003.

Bowen, Richard A. *The Italian Americans*. Broomall, PA.: Mason Crest, 2008.

D'Amico, Joan and Karen Eich Drummond. *The Coming to America Cookbook*. Hoboken, NJ: John Wiley & Sons, 2005.

Petrini, Catherine M. *The Italian Americans*. Minneapolis, MN: Lucent, 2003.

Websites

https://www.loc.gov/teachers/classroommaterials/ presentationsandactivities/presentations/immigration/italian3.html
Read about the immigration experience and look at period photographs in this online exhibit from the Library of Congress.

http://www.everyculture.com/multi/Ha-La/Italian-Americans.html
Get an overview of Italian history, culture, and immigration here.

http://www.fourpoundsflour.com/ living-history-eating-like-an-italian-immigrant-family-in-1919/
Follow along with one blogger's experiment eating like an Italian immigrant from a century ago.

http://www.pier21.ca/culture-trunks/italy/history
Learn more about the history of Italian immigration to Canada.

Series Glossary of Key Terms

acclimate   to get used to something

assimilate   become part of a different society, country, or group

bigotry   treating the members of a racial or ethnic group with hatred and intolerance

culinary   having to do with the preparing of food

diaspora   a group of people who live outside the area in which they had lived for a long time or in which their ancestors lived

emigrate   leave one's home country to live in another country

exodus   a mass departure of people from one place to another

first-generation American   someone born in the United States whose parents were foreign born

immigrants   those who enter another country intending to stay permanently

naturalize   to gain citizenship, with all its rights and privileges

oppression   a system of forcing people to follow rules or a system that restricts freedoms

presentation   in this series, the style in which food is plated and served

Index

Photo Credits

Author Bio

Diane Bailey has written more than 50 nonfiction books for kids and teens, on topics ranging from science to sports to celebrities. She also works as a freelance editor, helping authors who write novels for children and young adults. Diane has two sons and two dogs, and lives in Kansas.